D0602424

ABOUT THE BANK STREET READY-TO-READ SERIES

More than seventy-five years of educational research, innovative teaching, and quality publishing have earned The Bank Street College of Education its reputation as America's most trusted name in early childhood education.

Because no two children are exactly alike in their development, the Bank Street Ready-to-Read series is written on three levels to accommodate the individual stages of reading readiness of children ages three through eight.

○ *Level 1:* GETTING READY TO READ (Pre-K–Grade 1)
   Level 1 books are perfect for reading aloud with children who are getting ready to read or just starting to read words or phrases. These books feature large type, repetition, and simple sentences.

● *Level 2:* READING TOGETHER (Grades 1–3)
   These books have slightly smaller type and longer sentences. They are ideal for children beginning to read by themselves who may need help.

○ *Level 3:* I CAN READ IT MYSELF (Grades 2–3)
   These stories are just right for children who can read independently. They offer more complex and challenging stories and sentences.

All three levels of The Bank Street Ready-to-Read books make it easy to select the books most appropriate for your child's development and enable him or her to grow with the series step by step. The levels purposely overlap to reinforce skills and further encourage reading.

We feel that making reading fun is the single most important thing anyone can do to help children become good readers. We hope you will become part of Bank Street's long tradition of learning through sharing.

The Bank Street College of Education

For Bill Hooks
— E.S.

For Rosemary
— G.C.

Please visit our web site at: www.garethstevens.com
For a free color catalog describing Gareth Stevens' list of high-quality books and
multimedia programs, call 1-800-542-2595 (USA) or 1-800-461-9120 (Canada).
Gareth Stevens Publishing's Fax: (414) 332-3567.

Library of Congress Cataloging-in-Publication Data

Schecter, Ellen.
    The boy who cried "Wolf!" / retold in rebus by Ellen Schecter; illustrated by Gary Chalk.
      p. cm. -- (Bank Street ready-to-read)
    Summary: Uses rebuses to retell the Aesop fable about a young boy whose false cries for
help bring him to an unfortunate end.
    ISBN 0-8368-1691-9 (lib. bdg.)
    1. Rebuses. [1. Fables. 2. Rebuses.] I. Chalk, Gary, ill. II. Title. III. Series.
PZ8.2.S34Bo   1997
398.22--dc20
[E]   96-30699

This edition first published in 1997 by
Gareth Stevens Publishing
A World Almanac Education Group Company
330 West Olive Street, Suite 100
Milwaukee, Wisconsin 53212 USA

Printed in Mexico

3 4 5 6 7 8 9 05 04 03 02 01

The Boy
Who Cried "Wolf!"

Retold in rebus
by Ellen Schecter
Illustrated by Gary Chalk

A Byron Preiss Book

A W.... ;hing
)UP COMPANY

Long ago,

when the world was still wild,

there was a young  boy.

He earned his living

taking care of  sheep.

Every day, as the ⬤ sun rose,
the 👒 boy led the 🐑 sheep
from the 🏠 village.
He took them to
a big, green ☁ meadow
where the 🌱 grass
grew sweet and thick.

"Be sure to call for HELP
if a  wolf comes,"
his  master told him.
"All the  people in
the  village will run
to help you."

All day,

as the ◯ sun shone bright,

the  boy played his ⚞ flute

and kept watch

over the 🐑 sheep.

For nearby there was
a deep, dark  forest
full of hungry  wolves.
Silently and swiftly
the  wolves crept
among the  trees.

They watched the  sheep
with hungry eyes.

For maybe you know that
a  wolf likes nothing better
than a delicious dinner of
tender  lamb chops!

One very hot day,

the  boy grew tired

watching the  sheep

in the bright  sun.

It was so quiet

he could almost hear

the  grass grow.

To stay awake, the  boy
pretended he saw  wolves
in the  clouds.
He imagined the  wolves
creeping like shadows
into the grassy  meadow.

Then the  boy

had a wicked idea.

He jumped up and ran

toward the  village.

"HELP!" he cried.

"A  wolf is eating

the  sheep!"

The  boy's shouts rang
through the village.
"HELP! Wolf!"
all the people cried.
They ran to the meadow
as fast as they could.

But all they found
was the  boy
laughing so hard he could
hardly stand.
The  sheep were
safe and sound,
munching the sweet, thick  grass.

"But where is the  wolf?"
cried the  people.
"There is no  wolf,"
laughed the  boy.
"It was just a joke.
I wanted to see if you
would come."

All the  people
were very angry
as they turned back
toward the village.

"Don't ever do that again!"
scolded the  master.
"I won't," promised the boy.
But he kept on laughing
and laughing.

A few days later,
the  boy grew tired
of playing his  flute
and watching the  clouds.
He could barely keep
his eyes open.

Then he remembered what fun

he had watching

all the  people

run from the  village

to help chase away the  wolf!

The  boy jumped up
and ran to the  village.
"HELP!  Wolf!" he cried.
Once again all the  people
ran to help.

But again there was no  wolf.
The sheep were munching
the fresh, green grass.
And once again the boy
just laughed and laughed.

All the  people

mumbled and grumbled.

"Don't expect us to come again,"

they told the boy.

His master frowned.

"How can I ever trust you again?"

But the  boy
was laughing so hard
he couldn't hear a word.

Then one evening,
as the red  sun
set in the sky,
the  boy fell fast asleep.
Shadows crept out of
the deep, dark  forest.

And a real  wolf
crept out with them!
Suddenly the  wolf
jumped from the shadows
and attacked the  sheep.

The  boy awoke and ran

to the  village.

"HELP!  Wolf!" he shouted.

People heard him.

But they did not believe him.

"There is no  wolf," they said.

"HELP! Wolf!"
the boy cried again.

"How many times does
that boy think
he can fool us?"
 people asked.

The  people were tired
after working all day.
Some were eating their supper.
Others were rocking their babies.

"You won't catch us running
to help that liar!" they said.
Even the  boy's master
just yawned
and soaked his tired feet.

"HELP!  Wolf!"

the  boy cried once more.

All the  people heard him.

But this time no one believed him.

This time no one ran to help.

The  wolf
killed many  sheep
before it slipped back
into the  forest.
And all the  people
ever found of the  boy
was his little  flute.

So maybe now you see
why no one believes a liar...
even when he tells the truth.